Praise for the Business Writing Course

"The section on tips for better writing and communication skills was one of the best parts." PA, AstraZeneca, Spain

"The course gave me a boost of confidence that shows I am capable of drafting letters." Manchester United Football Club

"I learnt such a lot from the course, I take a bit longer over everything I write now, but it is amazing the difference if you change the 'tone' of the message." Business Writing for the Accommodation Team of the University of Salford

"I found the course very useful and geared to the industry I am in."

"I feel a lot more confident using punctuation. I found the course interesting and everything is explained clearly."

"I learnt how to deliver bad news with a positive spin."

"It is all great and adaptable for my role."

"I particularly found the practising of email writing and feedback given was incredibly helpful."

"I thought this was focussed and incredibly useful. The methods, hints and tips which I learned will enable me to improve the quality of my work."

"I would certainly recommend this course to others."

"Extremely informative."

"It is fantastic and has helped me improve my writing skills."

About the author:
Heather Baker

Heather had over twenty years' experience as a secretary and PA before setting up Baker Thompson Associates Limited in 2000. The company specialises in the training and development of secretarial and administrative staff (www.bakerthompsonassoc. co.uk). She now travels all over the UK working with large and small companies to enable their office staff and PAs to work more effectively and efficiently. She also facilitates courses in the Middle and Far East. Heather is a Certified NLP Practitioner.

She worked for ICI Pharmaceuticals (now AstraZeneca) and Hewlett Packard. She spent 5 years in France working for the Commercial Director of Cognac Hine and then 10 years with Granada Media working up to personal assistant to the managing director, commuting regularly between their offices in Manchester and London.

Heather conceived the speedwriting system BakerWrite and wrote the Amazon best selling book based on this system (Speed Writing skills training course, www.UoLearn.com) which is also offered as an online training course (www.bakerwrite.com). She is also the author of Successful Minute Taking.

She has been married to Ian since 1979 and they have two daughters, Ailsa and Erin.

Easy 4 me 2 learn

Bestselling books by Heather Baker

Successful Minute Taking, ISBN 978-1-84937-038-7

Speed Writing Skills Training Course, ISBN 978-1-84937-075-2

Order books from your favourite bookseller or direct from www.uolearn.com

Successful business writing

How to write business letters, emails, reports, minutes and for social media.
Improve your English writing and grammar.

Improve your writing skills. A Skills Training Course.
Lots of exercises and free downloadable workbook.

Published by: Universe of Learning Ltd, reg number 6485477, Lancashire, UK
www.UoLearn.com, support@UoLearn.com

First Published 2012

ISBN 978-1-84937-071-4, UK spelling edition

Other editions:
ebook pdf format 978-1-84937-072-1
epub 978-1-84937-073-8
US spelling printed version: 978-1-84937-074-5

Photographs © www.fotolia.com
Cover photo © Chagin and Elen studio, www.fotolia.com
Edited by Dr Margaret Greenhall.

Spelling chequer poem written by Jerrold Zar and reprinted with kind permission of The Journal of Irreproducible Results, www.jir.com

Successful Business Writing

Introduction

I am passionate about the English language. It has one of the richest vocabularies and a grammatical system that enables us to express the tiniest nuance of meaning; particularly of time.

Successive governments who decided teaching English grammar was no longer important have failed the children of those times. The ability to communicate – effectively – is a basic human right.

I am not concerned with being overly fastidious about phrases and grammar, particularly with the "we've always done it like this" view; I do think language should be allowed to evolve. If not, we would all still be speaking like Shakespeare (although is that such a bad thing?!). However, punctuation and grammar facilitate clarity and understanding; this should not be lost on a whim.

Lynne Truss, the author of Eats, Shoots and Leaves, makes a statement I love that punctuation enables the reader to "hum the tune". When somebody reads what you have written, they should almost be able to hear you saying it.

So, naturally, my passion crosses over into business writing; that has been my working life. It is pitiful to see so much badly written and ineffectively expressed correspondence. The lack of imagination and creativity can be deplorable.

This book has lots of exercises to help you learn the skills as you go through it. If you would prefer not to write in this book then please do visit www.uolearn. com and download the free workbook which has all the exercises in it.

I hope this book helps you, dear reader, to make the most of your natural skills ....

Flowchart for business writing

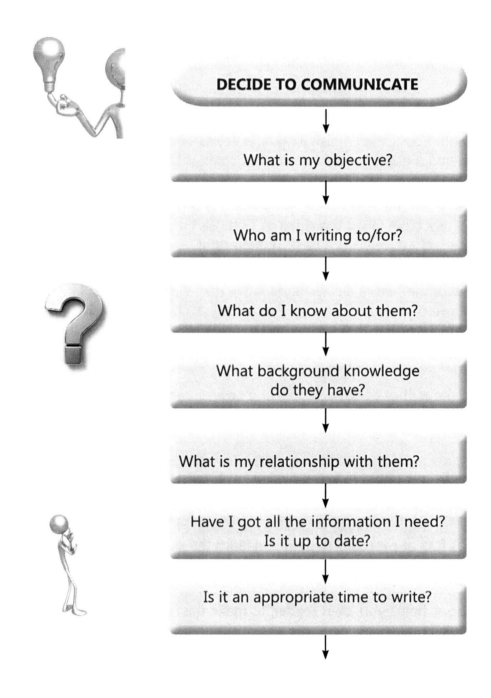

DECIDE TO COMMUNICATE

What is my objective?

Who am I writing to/for?

What do I know about them?

What background knowledge
do they have?

What is my relationship with them?

Have I got all the information I need?
Is it up to date?

Is it an appropriate time to write?

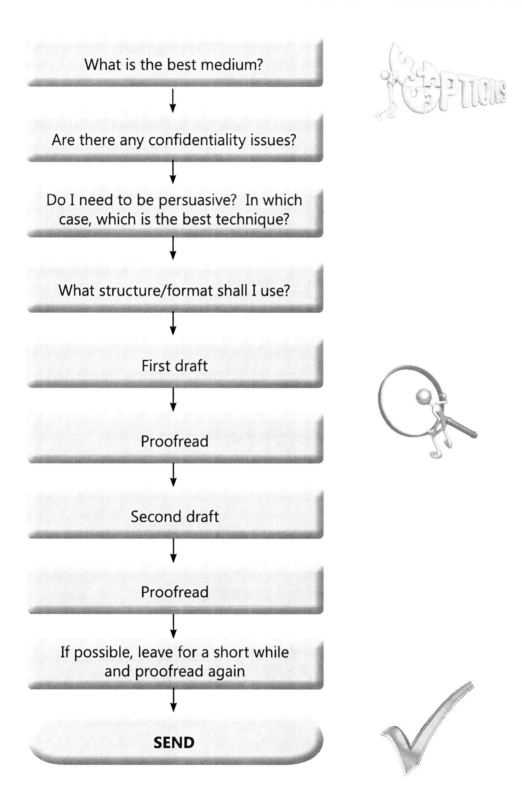

What is the best medium?

Are there any confidentiality issues?

Do I need to be persuasive? In which case, which is the best technique?

What structure/format shall I use?

First draft

Proofread

Second draft

Proofread

If possible, leave for a short while and proofread again

SEND

7

Contents

Chapter 1:
Why are good writing skills important in business?

"When something can be read without effort, great effort has gone into its writing." Enrique Jardiel Poncela

Chapter 1:
Why are good writing skills important in business?

In this chapter you will learn:

✓ Reasons to improve your business writing skills

✓ Barriers to excellent writing skills

You may be familiar with the Plain English Campaign (www.plainenglish.co.uk). Since 1979, they have been campaigning against gobbledygook, jargon and misleading public information. They have worked with many government departments and other official organisations with their documents, reports and publications. They believe that everyone should have access to clear and concise information – and I support them 100%.

Every year they give awards for the "best" examples of gobbledygook – the Golden Bull Awards. Here is one of the winners:

LSIS (Learning and Skills Improvement Service) from a consultation booklet 'Statement of strategic direction' sent to schools

The government calls insistently for more innovation. But doing things in a new way will not necessarily lead to better outcomes. So, what do we mean by innovation? We share the thinking of, for example, the Work Foundation, which sees innovation not "as a set of discrete and singular moments of change" but rather as "a culture or process in which drivers of change are embedded in and facilitated by the strategic outlook of the organisation."
To draw an analogy from nature, innovation may be thought of as 'the new season's growth' rather than a series of isolated 'bright ideas'.

What hope is there for the business world if leaders of education are writing such incomprehensible documents?

There are three principal reasons why good business writing is important:

➢ To communicate your ideas precisely and concisely

➢ To establish relationships

➢ To convey an excellent image of your organisation

1. Communicating your ideas precisely and concisely

With the advent of technology, we are writing so much more than, say, 15 years ago. I remember my then 7 year old younger daughter coming into work with me one day after she had had some teeth extracted. At school the next day she told her teacher she had been to work with mummy. "Oh, that's nice, Erin. What does mummy do?" Did my daughter impress her teacher with tales of my responsible role as PA to the Managing Director of Granada? Of course not – "she's on the telephone," Erin replied! But how true – in those days meetings were arranged by 20 or 30 phone calls; there was no email or meeting schedulers. I did, in fact, spend most of my day on the telephone.

11

Nowadays, meetings and most of our business tasks are carried out by email and the internet. Sadly, many people think that because email is "less formal" we have no need for the standards required in "formal" letters.

An email is simply a letter sent electronically.

Although the layout may differ, the same standards you would use for a letter should be applied to every email. It is still vital to be understood and it shows respect for your reader(s) to convey well written messages.

So much time can be wasted by the to-ing and fro-ing of emails because the writers have put little or no thought into their text. From a time management point of view this is very negative; it can also be costly. Just taking a couple of extra minutes to think and prepare before you click on SEND can be so much more efficient – and effective.

STOP BEFORE YOU SEND

2. Writing to establish relationships

When you are writing to someone you are building up a relationship with that person. Often you may never have met the person; perhaps they work in another building, another company or town and, of course, perhaps another country. Despite the lack of face to face contact, we develop working relationships and even friendships with each other through email.

If there is a lack of thought in how we express ourselves we can, unintentionally, upset or offend our reader(s).

In a face to face situation we are constantly picking up "messages" from each other; most of the messages we pick up from others come from their body language and people discover so much about us from how we stand, our gestures or our eye movements. The second way we understand people is through their tone of voice; do they sound nervous? Are they shouting or whispering? Only a small part of our understanding comes from the words people use – think in how many different ways you can say "I'm fine". The meaning comes from the tone of voice and body language, not the words.

Therefore, we have to be extremely carefully when choosing our words for business writing; our reader can't see the smile on our face or hear the laughter in our voice which can temper a slur!

[This book has lots of exercises to help you learn the skills as you go through it. If you would prefer not to write in this book (or it's not yours) then please do visit www.uolearn.com and download the free workbook which has all the exercises in it.]

> **With whom do you have "written relationships"?**
>
> ....
>
> ....
>
> ....
>
> ....
>
> ....

We will be looking at this in more detail later.

13

3. Conveying an excellent image of your organisation

Conveying your ideas precisely and laying out your documents effectively gives an image of you, the writer, as someone professional with high standards; this can impact on the general impression that colleagues and clients have of you. As well as improving your own career prospects, it can also improve the success of your business.

Clients will often select a supplier, for example, based on the professional look of their correspondence, the ease of reading their documents or the tone of their emails.

We'll be looking at how you can do this over the next few chapters.

Are there any other reasons in your organisation why you believe your writing skills are vital?

What are the barriers to good written communication?

➢ **Incorrect grammar, spelling and punctuation**

If sentences are not clear through incorrect grammar or misuse of punctuation then confusion can arise. Spelling mistakes just show a lack of care – which your reader may anticipate filters into the work you do.

➢ **Not considering your reader(s) – their language, culture, background and knowledge**

Misunderstandings can occur when corresponding with people whose first language is not English. Furthermore, a lack of understanding of your reader's culture and background can cause problems with building relationships as well as confusion. The use of technical expressions for a person who does not have the specialised knowledge means your writing is worthless.

➢ **Misjudging relationships**

Being too informal or too formal with a reader can lead to misunderstandings and even offence.

➢ **Not understanding the issues**

Don't write to somebody unless you totally understand the situation. Your lack of appreciation of the topic will always show through.

➢ **Tight deadlines**

In the busy world in which we work, we often have to produce documents or send emails at very short notice and with little time. This means less care may be taken, leading to many of the problems already mentioned.

➢ **Inappropriate words and/or tone**

Similar to misjudging a relationship, this can occur when a person hasn't thought about the impact of words they write or they use a tone that may cause offence.

➢ Being emotional

Never send an email or letter when you are angry or upset. Type a draft, of course; this can be quite cathartic. **But don't click on send.** Wait an hour or so, or, even better, overnight, and then decide whether or not to send. Your correspondence will have so much more impact if it is written objectively. Under no circumstances send emails or texts when you've had alcohol.

➢ Lack of preparation

Due to the simplicity and speed of email, people often just type and send. This can result in long exchanges, misunderstandings and not the best result for you, the writer. An extra bit of time putting some thought into your correspondence can make an enormous difference.

We're going to look at all these in more detail throughout the book.

> Are there any other specific barriers to good written communication within your work environment?
>
> ....
>
> ....
>
> ....
>
> ....
>
> ....
>
> ....
>
> ....
>
> ....

Chapter 2: Purpose of written communication

"If you don't know where you are going, you will probably end up somewhere else." Lawrence Peter

Chapter 2:
Purpose of written communication

In this chapter you will learn:

✓ Why planning and preparation are important
✓ Some basic reasons you may send written communications

For correspondence to be properly prepared and written, you need to clarify why you are sending the message.

This may be very simple you might send a message:

✓ To explain something
✓ To ask for something
✓ To answer a question
✓ To persuade

When I am training in business writing, these are some of the many reasons people give me when I ask why they send emails and letters. These are good, and correct, answers, but we need to think about this a bit more. Why do we need to explain? Why do we need to answer questions? If we keep asking the question, "but why?" we eventually get to the answer – to ensure the success of the organisation:

"Why do we need to explain to the new receptionist about the booking system?"

"To enable him to make the bookings correctly."

"Why?"

"So the system works and no mistakes are made."

"Why?"

"Because people will be unhappy."

"Why does that matter?"

"People should be happy at work."

"Why?"

"Because they are more productive."

"Why is that important?"

"To enable to organisation to be successful."

Why do you send correspondence or write documents?

If you can keep asking why, you may not have got to the real reason yet.

Every single email, letter, report or document you issue, whether internally or externally, contributes to your success and thus the success of the organisation. The same applies to every telephone call you make (look out for this in my next book).

For Want of a Nail

For want of a nail the shoe was lost.
For want of a shoe the horse was lost.
For want of a horse the rider was lost.
For want of a rider the battle was lost.
For want of a battle the kingdom was lost.
And all for the want of a horseshoe nail.

After thinking about why you need to send the communication you need to think of your objective.
What do you want to achieve?

Examples of objectives:

➤ I want to get a job interview.
➤ We need to get funding for the project.
➤ We need to ensure that the auditors can find all of the correct documents.

Think of a piece of either recent communication or one you're about to write.

Why are you writing?

....
....

Why?

....
....

Why?

....
....

Why?

....
....

Why?

....
....

What is your objective?

....
....

Some of the basic objectives might be:

To explain

We may be replying to a colleague's or client's query or we may be explaining to someone how to do something, why we do something or what a system is for – there could be hundreds of reasons.

Rather than just writing out our thoughts and sending an email, we should put ourselves in the place of the reader:

➢ Why does the reader need this information?

➢ Why do we want the reader to have this information?

➢ What do they know already?

➢ What do I think they don't know?

➢ What is confidential?

We should also try and anticipate any questions the reader may have and include the answers.

Furthermore, we need to think about the type of person we are writing to (see the following chapter).

To ask for something

Often we send emails to request information or favours. We could simply ask the question, but there are other techniques which may be more effective and so, again, this involves a little preparation.

➢ **Inspire**

Politicians and activists use this technique to incite or motivate. We can use it to encourage our reader to do something for us. For example, "If we get this quotation to the potential client as quickly as possible they will be really impressed with us and this could lead to great things for the organisation".

➢ **Flattery**

Politicians use this technique too! It's simply making your reader feel good. "You're really good at PowerPoint; could you help me with my presentation?"

➢ **Tit for tat**

This means simply offering to do something in return. "Could you possibly cover for me on Monday; I'll do Friday for you?"

➢ **Favour**

Sometimes we can't offer anything in return, but we could just be very grateful to someone for doing something for us. "Please" and "thank you" are essential.

➢ **Silent allies**

Silent allies are used by companies in advertisements. "9 out of 10 women preferred our lipstick." Testimonials are a type of silent ally. "We would like you to introduce the new system into your department; Finance and HR use it already and find it invaluable."

➢ **Authority**

This is simply using either your position of power (or your manager's) to get things done. Copying an email to someone's line manager is another example of this technique. Preferably use this as a last resort and never use force or blackmail; that would be considered work place harassment.

We take this further in chapter 9 on persuasive communication.

To answer an enquiry

If you are preparing to reply to someone's question, you should incorporate some of the techniques above. You should also think about your objective in answering the question, not just your reader's objective in sending the query.

Although for the majority of these chapters we are referring to emails and letters, your purpose may be to create something else.

For example you may be writing one of the following:

➢ Report

➢ Brochure

➢ Website

➢ Proposal

➢ Tender

➢ Social media

All of the same standards are applicable. We will look at these specific items later in the book.

So, once you've established your purpose, you can then start your preparation (remember, all this may only take 30 seconds). We are going to come back to more on your purpose later in the book.

Notes:

Chapter 3:
People

"I consider it a good rule for writing to leave unmentioned what the recipient already knows, and instead tell him something new." Sigmund Freud

Chapter 3:
People

In this chapter you will learn:

✓ What to consider about your reader(s)

So, we've gone through all our preparation and thought about why we are writing and who we are writing to. We've thought about our structure and got all the information we need. It would be very easy just to type up our thoughts, proofread and then send …. There are still a couple of things we need to think about and the first is not just who we are sending the message to, but also what is that person like? What are their preferences? What do we know about them? Is it just one recipient or more?

A message is most effective if it is tailored to the recipients.

Exercises: First of all, what do you know about your reader?

Think about emails or letters you send and list below what you think may be helpful to know about the recipients:

....

....

....

....

....

Here are some more suggestions:

Age

Although you may not know someone's age, and it shouldn't really make much difference anyway; it can help to know approximately when someone was born.

This can affect the type of references you may use and lets you know whether you are dealing with a technology native (grown up with it) or a technology immigrant (learned how to use it in later life). However, never assume or patronise.

Background to the situation

Make sure you know the history behind the correspondence you are to write. Go through files, talk to other people and look at previous correspondence.

Culture

What is your reader's background? Are they European, Asian, Middle Eastern, African, American, Australasian. Again, this doesn't always matter, but it does if you, in Europe or America, are writing about "the weekend" to someone in Saudi Arabia, where their weekend is Thursday and Friday.

Education

You may want to change some of the references or terms you use based on a person's training.

Gender

Obviously, in general, it should not make any difference if we are writing to a man or a woman. However, this may affect references that we make in our writing.

How busy they are

A very busy person, particularly high level management, will not want (and shouldn't want) emails full of detail. Give them bullet points, bottom line, summaries, key messages, all in a user friendly format.

How do they like to receive information?

Does your reader like to receive bulleted emails or separate messages for each topic? Do you think they may like a larger font (very helpful for the over 50s I can assure you!)?

How important is the message to them?

This communication may be vital to you, but may not be to your reader; you need to make them feel your urgency, see the section on persuasive communication.

If it is important to them and not to you, bear that in mind in your tone of writing; flippancy over something crucial to your reader will not be taken well.

Knowledge

Hopefully a doctor would not write to a patient using large amounts of medical terminology or a computer hardware manufacturer to a customer using technical jargon. Always take into account the general and specialist knowledge of your reader(s).

Language

Very simply, is English your reader's first language? If not, ensure your language is as straightforward as possible – without being patronising.

Remember to avoid sayings such as "taking coals to Newcastle" or "that's like bringing quahogs to the clambake" which don't translate very well to other cultures. In Germany they "take owls to Athens" or in France they "take water to the river".

Personality type

Some people like detail, some people like bullet points. Others care about what happens to people, some about what happens to systems. Always take into account the personality of your reader(s).

Position in the company

No matter to whom you write, you should always be polite, professional and respectful. Even so, you may write things in a different way (maybe more informally, but definitely not with lower standards) if you are writing to your colleague at the next desk rather than the managing director.

Relationship

Consider your relationship with the person(s) to whom you are writing. If you are too formal to a long-standing colleague, they may wonder if they have upset you! Alternatively, being too informal with someone you don't know could cause conflict.

Their preferences

"People will sit up and take notice of you if you sit up and take notice of what makes them sit up and take notice." (Frank Romer)

Their situation

Consider the situation your reader is in. Are they very busy, are they feeling unwell, have they had a bereavement? Do they have money issues etc? As I said previously, you can't always know these things, but the more you know the more you can tailor your correspondence.

Special needs

Does your reader need a larger font?
Do they have to have access to a speaking computer?
Have we considered any disabilities in giving people instructions or directions?
People with dyslexia may need a different colour of paper; older people and people with vision problems can be helped by printing black text on yellow paper.

Exercise: Who is your reader?

Is it one person or more?
How old are they?
What is the history behind the correspondence?
Where are they from? What is their first language? What is their culture?
What qualifications, knowledge, etc do they have?
Are they male or female?
What level are they within the organisation?
How busy are they?
How do they like to receive information?
How important is your message to them?
What is their personality type?
What is your relationship with them?
What are their preferences?
Do they have any special needs?

Chapter 4:
Preparation for writing

"The pages are still blank, but there is a miraculous feeling of the words being there, written in invisible ink and clamouring to become visible." Vladimir Nabakov

Chapter 4:
Preparation for writing

In this chapter you will learn:

✓ How to structure and layout your correspondence

A four point plan to structure your writing

Firstly, you should have a structure to the correspondence you are creating. Here is a four point suggestion for the structure:

1. Opening
2. Detail
3. What happens next?
4. Close

1. Opening

The opening is "Dear Susan" or "Dear Mr Jones". If you are unsure of someone's title (or gender), you could perhaps start "Good morning" or "Good afternoon". In a more relaxed relationship "Hello Fran" is quite acceptable. Try and avoid "hi" or "hiya" – you want to sound professional.
"Dear Sir" or "Dear Madam" may be used occasionally, but I would recommend you find out the name of the person to whom you are writing; it is much more persuasive.
You may then continue with "Thank you for your email of 20 May.". Be careful of using "Further to your email of 20 May" and then not continuing the sentence; a full stop after the date in this example would be incorrect.

2. Detail

The detail is the main body of your correspondence. This may be one paragraph or twenty paragraphs. Within this main body you must ensure structure too. Paragraphs should be in a logical order with a new one for each step or topic. Type your message up initially but then change the order if necessary. Remember, you want it to be easy for your reader to understand. They don't want a transcript of the chaos of your thoughts!
You may also structure your detail chronologically or in order of priority. You can use headings or numbering for even more clarity and it is advisable to keep paragraphs as short as possible to ensure your correspondence is "reader friendly".

3. What happens next?

What does your reader need to do, what are you going to do?

Examples might be:

➢ Let me know your thoughts.

➢ Do give me your comments.

➢ Let's discuss this at our next meeting.

➢ I will let you have the information by Friday.

4. Close

The close may be "Kind regards" or " Best wishes". In formal letters that start "Dear Sir" or "Dear Madam" you should always close with "Yours faithfully". Otherwise "Yours sincerely" is fine.

For emails we tend to use Kind regards or Best wishes, both of which are acceptable. Some people also use "Warm regards" or "Very best wishes". Do try and avoid the kr or bw that some people write; it's going into the realms of text-speak and comes across as though you can't be bothered.

> **Where would you put these phrases?**
>
> 1. I hope to hear from you soon.
> 2. We are pleased to inform you that our Banquet Suite is available on the dates you require.
> 3. Thank you for your letter of .....
> 4. I am pleased to enclose our latest catalogue.
> 5. Do let me know if you have any questions.

You then need to ask various questions:

- ➤ Who should be included in the recipient list?
- ➤ What do they need to know?
- ➤ What do they know already?
- ➤ What questions may they have?
- ➤ Do I have all the information of the history of this issue?
- ➤ Do I have the correct names, addresses and correct spelling?
- ➤ How urgent and/or confidential is the content?

Ensuring you have all the relevant information before you start means you will avoid a long chain of correspondence involving questions you hadn't anticipated. It also, again, makes you look so much more professional and is more efficient and effective.

Visual impact of your communication

Part of your preparation will also be to think about the visual impact of your letters, emails, reports, etc.

A letter can be laid out in your organisation's house style; an example could be:

```
                    COMPANY LOGO
              COMPANY NAME AND ADDRESS


Today's date
Name of addressee
Address
City
Postcode


Dear xx,
SUBJECT


Text....
Text....


Yours....




Your name
Your title
List of enclosures
```

Nowadays, it is acceptable and most simple to use blocked style; that is justifying all text to the left of your letter. We also recommend using open punctuation. This means not using commas at the end of address lines or after Dear Sir, etc.

However, appropriate punctuation is essential within the main body of the letter.

Emails

Emails, of course, have a standard layout, however, you can make yours much easier to read by increasing the font size, leaving a line between paragraphs and dividing your communication into short paragraphs. Do not resort to text language.

When sending emails or memos put some thought into the subject line. This can help your reader enormously - and you, if you need to refer back, at a later date, to messages you have sent. Just putting "**Meeting**" as your heading isn't always very useful. It would be better to make the subject **"Meeting to discuss the building maintenance project"** or "**Meeting of the finance team on December 2nd**".

You may also want to be more specific, this, again, can be very helpful to your reader – "**Options for refreshments at the finance meeting on December 2nd**".

Finally, ask yourself a question; is email the best way to send this message or should it perhaps be a telephone call, a letter or even a personal visit (if feasible)?

Doing something in business writing because "we have always done it like that" is just not acceptable.

Example email layout:

To: ANOther@xyz.com

cc:

Suject: SUMMARY OF MEETING ON 3 JANUARY

Dear Anne

It was a pleasure to meet you last week and here is a summary of the points we agreed:

1.   You will provide a report on the new product

2.   I will obtain information on costings

3.   I will arrange the training sessions.

Do let me know if you need more information.

Best wishes

Heather

It is also possible to insert standard signatures on all your emails, for example to give information about your organisation and your contact details. This is mine in 2012:

Heather Baker
Director
Baker Thompson Associates Limited
NEW http://www.bakerthompsonassoc.co.uk/cms/videos - watch an interview with Heather
www.bakerthompsonassoc.co.uk - ensuring PA/administrative excellence since 2000
http://www.bakerthompsonassoc.co.uk/cms/publications - order copies of Heather's books
NEW http://www.bakerwrite.com/cms/ – dedicated BakerWrite speedwriting website

To do this you must be in a new email and then produce the signature you want. In outlook you would then click on "insert", then "signature" and "signatures".   A dialogue box will appear and you can then create a new signature by inserting a copy (cut and paste) of your proposed text and giving it a name. These can be edited at a later date and you can also create alternatives with different names and text. Click on "OK" when you have finished.
Ideally, these should not be in a large font and certainly should be smaller than the body of the email.
Some things you might like to put on your signature:
➢ Name
➢ Job Title
➢ Company name
➢ Email address (in case your email gets forwarded on)
➢ Full telephone number
➢ Postal address
➢ Website
➢ Privacy information

Chapter 5:
Different forms of
written communication

"The best style is the style you don't notice."
Somerset Maugham

Chapter 5:
Different forms of written communication

In this chapter you will learn:

✓ About different types of communication including: emails, letters, minutes, reports, brochures, websites, tenders and social media

Emails

We are all familiar with the layout of emails and to ensure yours really impress, here are a few tips:

➤ Insert a blank line between paragraphs to make it easier to read

➤ Use a larger font than the standard one

➤ Always include a clear subject. Also, change the subject if the content is changing – although you may be better starting again or speaking on the 'phone or face to face.

➤ Make it easy to read

Here are some general suggestions for effective emails:

➢ Only copy and circulate appropriately – this saves your colleagues' and clients' time

➢ Be specific – plan exactly what you have to say

➢ Don't use text speak

➢ Get to the point

➢ Spellcheck/proofread

➢ Be professional

➢ Imagine you are talking to the person

➢ Don't forget that email is permanent

➢ Think before you forward

➢ Would a 'phone call be better?

➢ Delete as you reply

➢ Delete as you forward

➢ Delete when you print off

➢ Save in a file if you need a template

➢ Use colour coding (in Outlook you can format your emails to appear in different colours depending on who has sent them – this comes under automatic formatting)

➢ Daily file management

➢ Delete all junk and spam and unsubscribe

We waste a huge amount of time just deleting emails; unsubscribe yourself from mailshots you no longer need. It takes a few seconds more but then it's gone forever. I did this and within a week I had unsubscribed from 40 organisations – and my inbox was much more manageable.

I recommend Monica Seeley's book "Brilliant Email" for more general information about managing emails.

Letters

People do still write letters and here is a suggested simple layout:

BAKER THOMPSON ASSOCIATES LIMITED
Stockport
Cheshire

4 January 20XX

Mrs T Smith
Universe of Learning
Manchester

Dear Mrs Smith

Thank you so much for your enquiry; we would be delighted to help with the business writing skills training for your staff.

I will be at my desk all day on Friday and would be happy to talk to you on the 'phone about your specific requirements.

Kind regards
Yours sincerely

Heather Baker

Director

This style is called "blocked" as all the text is justified (or blocked) to the left-hand side.

Minutes

You can find out much more about notetaking, meetings and minutes in general in my book "Successful Minute Taking: Meeting the Challenge", order from www.uolearn.com.

When you have taken notes in a meeting and need to write your minutes, here are some tips to help:

➢ Follow the order of the agenda

➢ Summarise the meeting, don't type up everything that everybody says (minute taking is not dictation)

➢ Use 3rd person only and past tense

➢ Use reported speech

➢ Only include information that is relevant

➢ No matter in what order the discussions take place, you should always type the minutes in the order of the agenda. Minutes shouldn't be a complete rehash of the discussions; the document should be a reader friendly summary.

What is summarising?

It is writing concise minutes, not necessarily missing things out, but what you do write you write in as short a way as possible.

➢ **Identify key points**
As well as the basics such as date, time, location of meeting, attendees, apologies and details of next meeting, you should also always mention any papers that are discussed or tabled. Include any actions; anything that anyone has to do (including who has to do it and by when). Any decisions that are made should be minuted; anything that changes an existing situation or issue. Finally, always include anything that has to be kept on record for legal or company policy reasons.

Don't include examples or descriptions used simply to illustrate a particular point

When people speak they make a point and then usually give examples to illustrate that point. For the minutes you only need the key point.

Some of you may have read John Fowles' novels ("The French Lieutenant's Woman", "The Magus"); he is a very descriptive writer and, if someone walks through the door, he would probably describe the door frame, the door handle, etc. In fact, for the story, we only need to know that the guy has walked through the door. It is the same for minutes.

➢ **Arrange information into a logical order**

The minutes should always be written in the same order as the agenda, even if the meeting actually happened in a different order.

Also, within each agenda point, people will go in all directions with the discussion. Your notes may be in no particular order. When you come to type your minutes you should ensure your notes are well structured and logical. Nobody wants a rehash of the whole meeting.

Remember, you are not summarising in the meeting, you are taking notes in the meeting and summarising afterwards. If you've any doubt as to whether something should be included, just put it in your notes and decide later when you're calmer and have more time to think. Minute taking is not dictation.

You can also use a Livescribe smartpen to take notes. This computer in a pen records everything you write, hear or say (http://www.bakerwrite.com/cms/tools).

➢ **Keep to the facts – don't include opinions**

This is not you saying, "and I thought this was a load of rubbish!". This is where you use words that give away your opinion. For example, "there was a lengthy discussion". How long is "lengthy"? About 5 minutes on the afternoon before the weekend!

In an exercise about people taking examinations, that I did with my trainees, someone on my course wrote, "Mr Fish said that exams were looming." At no point was the word 'looming' used in the meeting. This just shows that the minute taker didn't like exams! Best of all, how about the person who wrote, "it was eventually decided"; how brassed off was that minute taker?

➢ **Check grammar, spelling, punctuation**

See later in the book for lots of advice on these.

➢ **Do not write in note form – use proper sentences**

I'm not saying don't use bullets; they are fine. However, you should write in full sentences, this is what gives your minutes clarity and elegance.

➢ **Avoid repetition**

It's important to vary vocabulary and we must also think about not using the same phrases more than once. Often, in a meeting, people will say things 3 or 4 times, possibly using different words. You may have some points in your notes more than once. When you come to write your minutes, make sure it's only in once.

➢ **Don't go through 'the process'**

This is what can make minutes extremely long-winded – see the following example:

The Chairperson said she needed a volunteer to get estimates for the new furniture in the office. She asked the Secretary to do this. The Secretary said she would do this. The Chairperson said she needed these for the next meeting. The Secretary said she would arrange this.

This could have been better written as follows:

The Secretary agreed to arrange estimates for the new furniture to be discussed at the next meeting.

Minutes should always be written in the third person; that is using he, she, it or they. You never use I or we in minutes as it is not a personal account, nor do you use you as you are not writing to someone.

You can also refer to the Chairperson, the Financial Director or Mr Smith and you can say the committee or they.

Another technique is using the passive; that is writing "it was proposed" rather than "Mr Smith proposed". This gives people some anonymity if required, although the writing style can become a bit heavy.

Minutes should always be written in the past tense as you are not writing about the situation at the moment (even if something is current). You are writing about what happened in the meeting. Remember these notes may be read a year or more later.

Imagine you are talking to somebody about what you did last night:

We went to the cinema, we had dinner at a restaurant and then we got a taxi home.

This is all in the past tense, so in minutes you would write, for example:

The committee agreed that the organisation did not have a good policy on health and safety and that, therefore, Mr Smith would look at what action should be taken.

Reported speech is the opposite of direct speech.

"I agree," said the chairperson is direct or quoted speech; this is not used in minutes. Instead we use reported or indirect speech:

The Chairperson said that she agreed.

Notice that when using reported speech we go back a step in time "I agree" becomes "she agreed"; we are reporting on something that happened in the past. If the chairperson had said, "I have already agreed to that", we would write "the chairperson had already agreed to that".

Reports/proposals

If you have to write a report for your business, here are some suggestions to help you:

➢ Keep to the facts

➢ Be objective

➢ Use 3rd person (see in the minutes section above)

➢ Ensure a good structure:

1. **Heading** – title of the report

2. **Terms of reference** – why you are writing the report (that is the objective of the report not "because my boss asked me to")

3. **Procedure** – how you obtained the information used in the report. Did you use questionnaires, have meetings? What books or reports did you read? Did you refer to internet sites, etc?

4. **Findings** – this should be set in paragraphs by topic, chronology or another logical sequence

5. **Conclusions** – a summary of your findings (there should be no new information here). This may sometimes be called an Executive Summary and be at the front of the report. It is a short version for people who don't need all the details.

6. **Recommendations** – only after you have presented all the findings do you offer your recommendations
Do not offer recommendations before your reader has all the facts, otherwise they don't have the best basis to evaluate those suggestions.

Before you start your report you should establish your objectives. Is the aim to:

- ➢ Inform
- ➢ Describe
- ➢ Explain
- ➢ Instruct
- ➢ Evaluate and recommend
- ➢ Provoke debate
- ➢ Persuade

It is important to establish who your readers will be.

> **Exercise: What do you know about your readers and their purpose for reading your report?**

To prepare you should gather your information which could come from other reports, meetings, discussions, research, internet, intranet, emails, questionnaires, experience, general knowledge, experiments, etc.

You should then sort the information into groups or under headings – flowcharts, lists or mindmaps can help you here.

Evaluate your information – are the findings reliable? Is the information strong, ie, does it stand up to debate, can it be proved by experiment, is it general knowledge? Always differentiate between fact and opinion.

It is also possible to mislead your reader by omission.

Ensure you only include relevant information and prioritise which information is most important.

Take this even further by reading Margaret Greenhall's book "Report Writing", order from www.uolearn.com.

Brochures

It is said that stimulating curiosity and capturing attention are the two main objectives of brochure copywriting. It doesn't matter how good your product or service is if you can't encourage interest from your brochure.

The later section on persuasive writing is very relevant to the text required for brochures.

Consider your reader and write what will capture their interest. Don't forget you need to include relevant and attractive images too.

For ideas on layouts search online for images of brochures. Collect any leaflets that you find in an ideas file. High quality images can be bought through sites such as www.shutterstock.com, www.fotolia.com and www.istockphoto.com. These can be used in any media without paying any more money. If you're using any images please check that you are following copyright rules.

Think about the size of the brochure - where will it be displayed and handed out?

Make sure the relevant contact details are on the brochure and proofread them very carefully. Write them out separately and ask someone else to check them too.

Check list for contact details:

- ✓ Contact name
- ✓ Company name
- ✓ Address
- ✓ Telephone number
- ✓ Email address
- ✓ Website/ social media

For most brochures it is important to keep text to a minimum. They are usually just the first step to getting a result.

Remember the most important part of your brochure is:

What action do you want the person to take?

Make sure it's clear how they can do this. Most people don't keep brochures so you need to make it easy for them to take the next step. In big letters email us... fill in this form... visit your doctor... bring this voucher to our office etc.

One of the most important parts about a brochure is the headline. This is what will entice people to pick it up, keep it or take action. Get a book like "Words that Sell by Richard Bayan and write at least 100 headlines. Keep going and then choose the best with a friend. Often writing a headline as a question will engage interest.

Consider a brochure as a starting point. Not all the information has to be on the leaflet itself. Often it's better to have a well designed visual brochure and a way of getting further information such as a website.

Make sure your fonts and layout are consistent throughout the brochure. Most design and word processing software have styles and formatting so you can set up different styles for your titles, text and images. A tip - if you use a table to make a folded leaflet set up thin blank columns where the folds will go to make sure the text doesn't get stuck in the fold. Word has lots of brochure templates - when you open a new file have a look on the left at the available templates.

Websites

Your website is your "shop window" and as with all other business documentation, it should be totally professional.

The one different element with websites is that you have to consider keywords that people might use to find your site. It is vital to include words that will be easily found through search engines. You need to repeat these keywords several times on the page.

Using the services of a professional web designer is advantageous.

The best way to think about writing a website is to remember people are looking for information but they spend very little time on each page so you need to write as though it were a newspaper. Have a thought provoking headline then stack the information with the most important at the top and the least at the bottom. Newspaper writers can have the last few centimetres chopped off their column and it still needs to make sense.

Decide what action you want your reader to take. Do you want them to buy straight away, change their lifestyle, remember the information or perhaps share their email? Then make it very clear what how they take that action. Give them several opportunities in different formats.

Search engine optimisation (SEO) is the term for making your site appeal to the search engines. There are lots of good books on this but some simple advice is:

➢ Think about the keywords your customers will use to search
➢ Use these about 5 times in the text
➢ Pick the most probable keywords and put them in the file name
➢ Put descriptive titles (alts) on all images
➢ Get as many links inward to the page as possible

Tenders

Writing a tender has many similarities to writing a report or a proposal, but let's look at some specifics.

Having established that you want to tender for some business, you need to decide what to include. Most importantly, focus on what the client needs and how you can help. If the client wants information in a specific format, use it.

Consider issues such as pricing, copyright, contracts, risks, resources.

For your preparation you should anticipate what questions the client may ask and ensure you can answer these in advance.

Things to include

➤ The purpose and origin of the bid

➤ Your work experience and credentials

➤ How and when the work will be carried out, delivery, etc

➤ Your team's skills and experience

➤ Management of the project

➤ Benefits of your bid

➤ Prices

➤ Potential challenges

It is also good to attach a covering letter which summarises your bid.

As for reports and all other documents, maintain high standards of spelling, grammar, punctuation and layout. Getting a tender professionally bound can just add the extra class to your bid. Make sure it arrives on time!

Social media

Finally, we should now also include social media. Again, as with email, this can be considered informal communication and therefore standards may drop. Everything we have said in this book should also apply to business writing on social media and the web.

Social media sites give a picture of you and your business; everything you write on there should be professional and of a high standard. Do not mix your business and personal pages (although occasional personal references on a business page can give a more "human" picture of you). Ensure you outline your business, skills and experience as fully as possible and, when letting people know what you can offer, make it sound as interesting and valuable as possible. If you just list your tasks this may not capture others' interest. If, however, you tell them how you can improve their lives, you will have a lot of interest!

It is also important with social media to give as well as take. Join discussions, offer advice, ask questions too.

Being as concise as possible is essential, nowhere more so than on Twitter. However, just because you are limited to 140 characters doesn't mean you should drop standards; just be clever with your use of words, punctuate and spell correctly and include links to give more information where appropriate.

Your tweets should fascinate and engage your reader; it shouldn't sound like an advertisement and yet should work as a sales pitch. It's also ideal if you can encourage people to retweet your messages so try not to use all your characters to allow for that.

Notes:

Chapter 6:
Writing good English

"Then there's the joy of getting your desk clean, and knowing that all your letters are answered, and you can see the wood on it again." Lady Bird Johnson

Chapter 6:
Writing good English

In this chapter you will learn:

✓ Grammar tips

✓ How to use punctuation

✓ How to use a good vocabulary

A good mastery of English

The first way to ensure your correspondence is effective is to use correct grammar and spelling.

Many people have been let down by successive governments who decided teaching grammar was no longer necessary. Grammar enables us to express our meaning precisely and with clarity; it is vital. It ensures we give a professional impression and time is saved because there is total understanding. Relationships are successful because offence is never caused. Your organisation looks good.

For more help with this try
Write Right!, Jan Venolia, ISBN 9781580083287
Mastering English Grammar, S.H.Burton, ISBN 9780333363683
Idiot's Guide to Grammar and Style, L.Rozakis, 9780028619569

So let's go over some of the basics that people get wrong.

Answers to most of the exercises in this section are at the back of the book.

Grammar

A verb is a doing word, eg, to dance, to eat, to have, etc.

Verbs usually go after the name of the person or object that is undertaking the action.

Eg: Peter **went** home on his motorbike.
Tina **was washing** her windows.
He **jumped** on the trampoline.

In the basic (or infinite version) you use the word "to" in front of the verb.

to walk, to see, to climb, to say

Verbs change their endings depending on what is undertaking the action and when it happened. They are often accompanied by parts of the verb to be (is, was, were). The three endings for regular verbs (ones that follow the rules) are:

s , ing and ed

I open the door. Paul open**s** the door. Hamid open**ed** the door. Sid **is** open**ing** the door. Sarah **was** open**ing** the door. Every sentence must have a verb. Sometimes, in modern text layouts, bullet points are used where the verb is given at the start and not included in each bullet point, but there should still be a verb. E.g.

We need to consider:

- The past year's accounts
- The current income
- Next year's projected income

Another important point about verbs is that the tense (which part of the verb to use) should be consistent throughout. If you look at the following you'll see how it doesn't work.

I **went** to a meeting and I **am buying** the materials from it. I **met** Sandra. She **is telling** me that there **is** another meeting next month.

This is clearly about an event in the past so all the verbs should agree and be about the past. So it should read:

I **went** to a meeting and I **bought** the materials from it. I **met** Sandra. She **told** me that there **will be** another meeting next month.

If you are writing minutes or reports they will usually in the past tense. The only parts that will not be are predictions about future actions. None of it should be in the present tense.

Once you've written your correspondence you need to check that the verbs are correct. One of the best ways to of this is to read it out aloud. (Try this with the example above.) Unfortunately grammar checkers may not pick it up.

An adverb describes how a verb was done.

He walked **quickly**. The rain was falling **heavily.**

A noun is a naming word this covers a wide variety, eg, table, Manchester, he, she, life, feeling, etc

Nouns are often preceded by a, an (if they start with a vowel) and the.

the house, a mouse, an elephant,

When writing you need to ensure that it is clear which person or object you are referring to. So sometimes it is appropriate to use impersonal pronouns (ones that don't repeat what the noun is) such as he, she, they or it. However, you need to be careful that the reader can work out who you mean.

Bad example: MJ said that PL should have found the accounts from last year. **He** said that this was an important task and that he would do it.

So now, who has agreed to do the task MJ or PL? It could be either of them. If more than one person is involved it is usually better to repeat the name of the person involved.
MJ said that PL should have found the accounts from last year. **PL** said that this was an important task and that he would do it.

Nouns should only start with capital letters if they are the name of a specific object or person (proper nouns).

For example, London, New York, July, John.

Capitals should not be used for emphasis only.

Adjectives describe nouns, such as colours and size.

The **blue** sky was above a **large** tree.

For many of the exercises in the good English section the answers are at the back of the book.

> Exercise: Pick out the verb(s), noun(s) and adjective(s) in the following sentences.
>
> 1. The usual chairperson read the minutes.
> 2. It was agreed to increase the annual salaries.
> 3. Mr Smith volunteered to send an explanatory email.
> 4. KL said that he would try out the new system.

Problem words:

Many of the words people struggle to spell have two variants with similar sounding alternatives and to make matters worse UK and US spellings can be reversed.

Examples of this are practice/practise and license/licence. As a rule of thumb, look for the use of 'the' and 'a' for a noun and 'ing' and 'ed' endings for a verb.

A really good way to remember other alternatives is to develop a strong memory for the correct spelling by making a connection between the correct spelling and something that makes sense to you (see the next page for some examples).

Words often spelt incorrectly:

Accommodation	Effect, usually noun	Practice (noun)
Accomplish	Environment	Practise (verb, UK)
Achieve	Further	Preferred
Acquire	Government	Receive
Address	Guarantee	Recommend
Affect (verb)	Immediately	Referred
Business	Independent	Separate
Colleague	Liaise/liaison	Stationary (not moving)
Commitment	Licence (noun, UK only)	Stationery (paper)
Committee	License (verb)	Success
Comparative	Necessary	Unforeseen
Conceive	Occasion	Withhold
Consensus	Opportunity	
Correspondence	Permanent	

A tip for UK spellers - if you're trying to decide c or s in practice or licence then try saying the words advice and advise instead. They work the same way as practice/practise. In the US practice and license are only spelt in this way.

Some examples of how you can remember some of these spellings:

affect = verb, How will this affect us?
I was affected by the music. The noise was affecting my performance

effect = noun (usually), The effect was serious. An effect of these problems is....

station**a**ry = not moving; not **active**
station**e**ry = papers, pens, etc (remember e for **envelope**)

princi**pal** = head of something, e.g. school principal, a person could be your **pal** also means the main reason
princi**ple** = an idea, an **excellent** idea

compl**e**ment = it **completes** something
compl**i**ment = a nice comment, use a compliment to **impress**

If you visit http://www.askoxford.com/betterwriting/spelling/?view=uk you'll find lots more useful tips.

Exercise: Are there any words you know you always mix up? If so, look up the correct version and think of a memory link to help you remember the spelling.

....
....
....

Exercise: Select the correct spelling from the options given in these sentences:

1. He had been practising/practicing medicine for years.
2. It was a nice compliment/complement about my work.
3. The principal/principle reason why the project succeeded was the team management.
4. The chairperson was concerned about the affect/effect this would have on the practise/practice time.

Punctuation

➤ Full stop (.)

A full stop used at the end of a sentence and is always followed by a capital letter. In the past, full stops were placed after all abbreviations; nowadays they are rarely used. This is called open punctuation. We know what 'etc', 'ie' or 'Mr' are.

➤ Commas

A comma (,) - denotes a pause in a sentence and can be used to break up items in a list.

If you write a list, all of the items should be separated by commas apart from the last two which should have and between them:

Our business last year sold widgets, gadgets, shapes **and** thingamabobs.

If you are writing long sentences then commas separate clauses. A clause is a part of the sentence that could be removed and the sentence still make sense. A clause usually gives more detailed information. There needs to be a comma at the start and end, unless the clause ends the sentence.

Examples:

At the meeting, **which was on Friday,** we decided to go ahead with project. **However,** it was decided that it wouldn't start until February.

So you could remove the clauses to get:

At the meeting we decided to go ahead with project. It was decided that it wouldn't start until February.

Which still makes sense.

What's the difference between a cat and a comma?
A cat has claws at the end of its paws and
a comma is a pause at the end of a clause!

➤ **Colons (:)**

Colons are used to denote the start of a list, often where the items within it are more than one word long. Traditionally after a colon all the items in the list are separated by semi-colons(;). However, modern usage is that they are often used to start bullet lists and the end punctuation is often not put in.

Traditional

There are four reasons for the project working: the team worked well together; the price of widgets rose; the price of electricity fell and none of the equipment failed.

Modern

There are four reasons for the project working:
1. The team worked well together
2. The price of widgets rose
3. The price of electricity fell
4. None of the equipment failed

➤ **Semi-colons (;)**

Semi-colons are used to separate complicated lists (see above). They can also be used to denote two separate thoughts in the same sentence; if in doubt, use a full stop. Often they replace conjunctions such as "and" or "but".

➤ **Exclamation marks (!)**

Exclamation marks should be used to denote surprise in a voice. He said, "Watch out!" However, they are now often used to denote irony and humour. In formal writing the advice is not to use exclamation marks at all.

➤ **Questions marks (?)**

Should be used to denote an asked question.

➤ **Brackets (())**

Brackets can be used as an alternative to commas, often they indicate an extra thought associated with but not necessary to the sentence, such as (see the previous letter).

➢ **Apostrophes (')**

The apostrophe is perhaps the most misunderstood of all punctuation and yet can be vital to complete clarity.

The apostrophe has 2 functions:

1. Contractions

2. Possession

Contractions

The apostrophe is used to indicate the missing letter(s), eg:

She's told him = She has told him

I'm here = I am here

I can't = I cannot

I wouldn't = I would not

We aren't = We are not

Words to watch out for:

your = belonging to you
you're = you are

there = over there
their = belonging to them
they're = they are

its = belonging to it
it's = it is or it has
(its' does not exist)

If you are not sure which to use try replacing **it's** by **it is** if it works you need the apostrophe, if it doesn't you don't need one.

It's finished now. It is finished now.

Its door was red. It is door was red - this doesn't work so no apostrophe is needed - the door belonging to something was red.

However, contractions are not usually used in very formal business writing.

Possession

When the possessor is single (ie, just one person or thing), we indicate possession by using an apostrophe followed by the letter s:
The director's report
My manager's project
The lady's desk

When the possessors are plural (ie, more than one person or thing), we indicate possession by placing an apostrophe after the final s:
The executives' conference
My colleagues' attitude
The secretaries' desks

However, when a word changes completely in the plural, the apostrophe remains before the s:
The men's books
The children's facilities
The women's bags.

If the subject is followed by a verb an apostrophe will probably not be needed, if it is followed by a noun then one may be required.

If you have a word with an s in it and you're not sure whether it needs an apostrophe try replacing the s with the words belonging to and put the noun first.

The director's car.
The car belonging to the director.
So, the apostrophe is needed as this works.

The directors sat in the car.
The car belonging to the directors sat in.
This makes no sense at all so the apostrophe is not needed, the s here just means more than one director. Also car is a noun and sat is a verb.

Apostrophes are not required where there is no possession eg:

The PAs visited the seminar.
The PCs were working well.
She was born in the 1960s.

Exercise: Add any missing apostrophes.

1. The clients rooms are nearby. (three clients)

2. The managers response was "no". (one manager)

3. The secretaries attitude must improve.

4. The mens preference was to sit down.

5. The caretaker says that hes happy with this plan.

6. Youre not sure what your choice will be.

7. Its difficult to know if the company and its representatives are included.

8. The SATs were very difficult.

A good vocabulary

There are different aspects of vocabulary that are important in business writing. You need to have a good variety of words that you can use so that you are not always repeating the same ones. You also need to have a working vocabulary for your specialist area.

Always use a thesaurus to vary your words and a dictionary to check that you are not altering the meaning of the text. Good online versions are www.thesaurus.com and www.yourdictionary. com.

> **Re-write the following paragraph making it flow better and sound more formal.**
>
> Jane said that there was a very good chance that the manager would tell the department what she was going to do. Linda said that the CEO had said that everyone should be told about the fact that there could well be redundancies.
>
> She also said that she thought this would happen.

Know your own in-house vocabulary

Any working environment has its own special words and acronyms or abbreviations (letters that represent something like NATO or USA) and an effective business writer you must use and understand these terms.

If they are more widely used acronyms you can use something like www.acronymfinder.com to help. However, if they are local terms then you've only got one option:

If you don't know ask!

The best way to approach this is to develop your own personal dictionary or make sure you cultivate curiosity and find out as much as possible about your organisation's business.

How might you do this?

1. Speak to colleagues and/or managers

2. Read emails, reports, etc

3. "Ears and eyes" – listen into conversations, watch what is happening around you

4. Use the internet (ensuring the sites are reliable) or your organisation's intranet

5. Media – radio, television, newspapers, journals

> **What specifically could you do in your work situation?**
>
> ....
>
> ....
>
> ....
>
> ....
>
> ....

Chapter 7:
Guidelines for good writing

"The time to begin writing an article is when you
have finished it to your satisfaction. By that time
you begin to clearly and logically perceive what
it is you really want to say." Mark Twain

Chapter 7:
Guidelines for
good writing

In this chapter you will learn:
- ✓ How to use short sentences, avoid wordiness and ambiguity
- ✓ How to use an appropriate tone and be precise
- ✓ How to check consistency

These are the guidelines we are going to cover:

1. Use short sentences
2. Avoid wordiness and choose simple words
3. Check for ambiguity
4. Use an appropriate tone
5. Be precise
6. Check consistency
7. Ensure accuracy

1. Short sentences

If sentences are too long you are much more likely to make grammatical mistakes, you will also lose your reader (as they fall asleep with boredom!). A Golden Bull Award winner had 630 words in one sentence, (see http://www.plainenglish.co.uk/awards/golden-bull-awards/golden-bull-winners-2005.html)

Where possible, your sentences should be no more than two or three typed lines (about 18-30 words). Remember to use commas to separate phrases.

> Here is an exercise to practise this. Insert punctuation and capital letters as you think appropriate. There are various options but, most importantly, it must make sense.
>
> At the meeting today the Chief Executive Mr John Smith suggested that a training course should be held for all sales staff members agreed that a two day seminar would be most appropriate it will be held in October it is therefore important that you and I should meet to decide on topics suggestions for speakers will also be needed of course your expertise and help in making the arrangements will be very valuable please let me know when it will be convenient for us to meet any afternoon next week would be suitable for me
>
> ....
> ....
> ....
> ....
> ....
> ....
> ....
> ....

2. Avoid wordiness and choose simple words

Be as concise as possible

Often in business correspondence we feel the need to "fill the page". Of course, this is no longer necessary and yet, I still see messages full of redundant words and phrases and full of waffle.

> **Improve these very wordy sentences:**
>
> 1. Please be informed that these statements will be dispatched to you on 12 July.
>
>   ....
>
>   ....
>
> 2. Please be informed that I will be unable to accept your invitation on this particular occasion.
>
>   ....
>
>   ....
>
> 3. We have pleasure in enclosing herewith a copy of our latest terms and conditions for your perusal.
>
>   ....
>
>   ....
>
> 4. I am in receipt of your letter of 8 January which we received today.
>
>   ....
>
>   ....

Don't use long words or phrases if shorter ones are available.

If a long word or phrase is the best option then use it; if there is a short, adequate word or phrase, use that. For example, why say commence when you could say begin or start? Or terminate instead of end. If you would have to use end twice in a sentence then use terminate to vary your vocabulary and avoid repetition but otherwise there is not really any need.

Find alternative ways of saying the following (using less or shorter words):	
Come to a decision	
In the event that	
Commence	
Terminate	
At the present moment in time	
Due to the fact that	
It is possible that	
It is probable that	
For the purpose of	

As mentioned earlier, do try and avoid repetition!

Use a Thesaurus to find alternative words. If you don't have one handy you can use the automatic Thesaurus within the word processing application. Simply select a word (by double clicking on it), right click in the highlighted area and you will be given a shortcut menu. Select "synonyms" and it will either offer you options or give you a short cut to the main thesaurus. One thing to note though, do check you are using the proposed word in the correct context - use your dictionary too.

3. Check for ambiguity

It is very easy to be ambiguous in our correspondence. We often just type out our thoughts and then send a message.

Stop before you send.

Always check before you send that the message will be clear to you reader. Although you know what you mean, your audience may not.

> Have a look at these examples of unclear extracts from documents and (using your imagination) make them into clear unambiguous sentences:
>
> 1. The shark-spotting helicopter apparently failed to see the shark, although it was circling over the bathers.
>
> 2. As the man went about his duties he watched him closely, noting the time he came to feed him.
>
> 3. I told my manager that she should help her.
>
> 4. If the baby doesn't like cold milk, boil it.
>
> 5. There are some plasters in my desk, which I keep for emergencies.
>
> 6. The car was in the garage when I painted it.

4. Use an appropriate tone

Let's have a look now at the tone you should use. Here is a variety of ways of saying the same thing in different tones.

➤ Sit down!

➤ Will you please sit down.

➤ Please sit down.

➤ Would you care to take a seat?

"Sit down" is very abrupt, rude and inappropriate in any business situation. It is not professional ever to show anger or bad manners.

At the other end of the scale, "would you care to take a seat" is rather sycophantic and I would avoid this "toady" tone.

Business writing should be at the "please sit down" point; always polite, not critical (or toady) and short and simple.

You may occasionally go to the "will you please sit down point" if you are "Disappointed of Stockport" in a letter of complaint, for example.

> Have a look at these inappropriately toned sentences written to clients or colleagues, decide why you think they are wrong and write them in a more professional way:
>
> 1. You have deliberately failed to reply to my letter.
>
> 2. We cannot do anything about your problem, try calling a solicitor.
>
> 3. Your interview will be held on Tuesday 20 May at 1400 hours.
>
> 4. The problem would not have happened if you had transferred the funds properly in the first place.
>
> 5. Your policy has expired so you'll have to pay for the repairs.
>
> 6. It's not our fault your DVD player doesn't work. You obviously didn't wire it up correctly.

It is inappropriate to tell a client that they have done something wrong, however, we need to help them with their problem and it may well be their fault.

The best way to achieve this is by using a technique that I call "floating in the air". We do this by suggesting a possible cause of a problem rather than accusing them of causing the problem (see the answers to the above for examples).

Finally on tone, make sure you are not being too formal or informal ....

Formal writing is less personal and more objective than informal writing.

Formal writing:

➢ Avoid slang
➢ Don't use contractions (e.g., don't, can't)
➢ Often uses third person (he, she, it, they – never I, you or we)
➢ The passive is used more than the active (e.g., instead of writing "we are concerned that" you may write "there has been concern that")
➢ Remain objective, don't be emotional

Informal writing:

- ➢ Use shorter sentences
- ➢ More likely to be in the first person (I, me)
- ➢ Exclamation marks (!) are acceptable

Here are some examples of how the same message could be sent:

In a formal way:

Dear Mr Jones

Thank you for your email about our meeting next week. I was sorry to hear that you are not well and quite understand why you had to postpone.

Do let me know when you are ready to rearrange our discussion and I hope you soon feel better.

Best wishes

Heather

Informally:

Dear John

Thanks for letting me know you aren't well and have to postpone our meeting.

Get well soon and let me know as soon as you are ready to rearrange our chat.

Best wishes

Heather

Although the text is shorter and more informal language and grammar are used, a high standard of writing is still maintained (ie, spelling, grammar, full sentences, etc).

5. Be precise

Do try not to be too vague in your correspondence (unless you actually don't want to be too specific for any reason). Rather than, "we'll get back to you in due course", you could say instead, "we'll get back to you within 7 days". It's more helpful to your reader.

You may want, or need, to be vague because you genuinely don't know when you'll be able to get back to someone. Alternatively, you may, for political reasons, not want to be too precise as a situation may change.

Avoid phrases like "as soon as possible" and "at your convenience".

Always give the day and date when you are making arrangements; this is a double check that it's completely correct and gives your reader more specific information, eg Friday 5th May.

Give precise information and details.

6. Check consistency

Are you writing from "I" or "we"? Keep it consistent. If you're using twelve hour clock, stick to that, don't mix it with twenty-four hour times. Be consistent with the way you write numbers, currency, distances, etc.

Ensure the information in your correspondence is also consistent throughout.

Use a consistent tone throughout (see above).

Generally we should write all single digit numbers (one to nine) and use figures above that (10 onwards). However, don't mix figures and words in the same text.

Ideally, don't start a sentence with a numeral; either put it in letters or change the word order, particularly for larger numbers:

- ✗ 30,000 people attended the match.
- ✓ Attendance at the match was 30,000.

Don't forget to check consistency of fonts, headings and all other layout issues.

7. Ensure accuracy

Always check the accuracy of your correspondence and that brings us to our next chapter .....

Chapter 8:
Proofreading

"Proofread carefully to see if you any words out." Author Unknown

Chapter 8:
Proofreading

In this chapter you will learn:

✓ The basic tools of proofreading

✓ What to check for

✓ Tips and common mistakes

Proofreading is an art as well as a skill. Although there are some basic rules, personal preference can play a large part in making decisions about the accuracy of a document.

Why is it important? Well, just like business writing skills generally, you want to give a good image of yourself and your organisation, you want to ensure clear communication and you want to build effective relationships. It is all part of the process. It can also be costly; I remember a delegate on a proofreading session I was facilitating for a UK local council. We were chatting about their objectives for the training and this man said he was there because he'd "been sent". Oh dear, I thought … it turns out he had not proofread a leisure services document correctly and had not noticed that the price for swimming should have been more. This had gone to the printers and, because it then became the published price, that was the price that had to be charged. He apparently lost the council tens of thousands of pounds that year.

Furthermore, proofreading is not just about checking figures and spelling – there is so much more; read on ....

Firstly, you need some basic tools:

➢ A fine-nibbed pen (rather than a blobby biro!) or sharp pencil – 2H is ideal

➢ A good eraser

➢ Learn how to use "track changes" in the word processing system. (Under the review tab you select the icon "track changes" and this will mean all your alterations to a document will be highlighted. In this way, other people can see how you have changed your text and they can they accept or reject changes.)

➢ A good source of natural light is preferable but, if not possible, ensure the overhead lighting is good

➢ A comfortable, quiet, uncluttered work environment – this is often not possible in a busy office, but you can try; perhaps there is a meeting room free

➢ Good eyesight – have regular check-ups and use your glasses or wear your lenses if you need them

➢ A ruler or a piece of paper to keep your eye focussed on the line you are reading – it is very easy to miss a couple of lines, particularly if the same word comes twice in a paragraph

➢ A calculator for checking tables, charts and figures

➢ Dictionary, thesaurus and the internet for reference

➢ Another person, if possible

Do you need any other tools for your checking?

I mentioned earlier that proofreading is not simply checking spelling, here is a list of some of the things you may need to look out for:

➢ Page numbers
➢ Copyright
➢ Headings
➢ Captions
➢ Headers and footers
➢ Dates
➢ Spacing
➢ Formatting
➢ Grammar
➢ Consider your audience
➢ House style and presentation
➢ Acronyms/abbreviations
➢ Inappropriate language
➢ Layout
➢ Numbering of footnotes
➢ Spelling
➢ Names
➢ Punctuation
➢ Titles (consistency and spelling)
➢ Fonts
➢ Widows and orphans*
➢ Website key words
➢ Content

We'll look at some of these in more detail later.

*Widows are where the last line of a paragraph is on the next page and orphans are where the first line is alone at the end of a page correct this automatically as follows:

1. Select the paragraphs in which you want to prevent widows and orphans.

2. On the Page Layout tab, click the Paragraph Dialog Box Launcher, and then click the Line and Page Breaks tab.

3. Select the Widow/Orphan control check box.

Note: This option is turned on by default.

What specifically may you have to check for in your job?

So, we've thought about the tools we need and what we have to check for, now let's look at some other hints to help you:

➢ Ideally, don't be tired – although clearly this is not always possible given deadlines

➢ Read slowly and carefully – it's easy to read and suddenly realise you've not actually been concentrating!

➢ Don't check for everything at once; go through looking for obvious spelling, grammar or text mistakes and then go through a few more times checking for specific things

➢ Read more quickly later to check for the sense

➢ After typing a document, leave it and go back to it later – this is similar to giving it to someone else to read; fresh eyes

➢ Always print off long documents; it's easier to spot errors However, I may be writing this as a "technology immigrant" (someone who remembers a time when we didn't have computers) as opposed to a "technology native" (someone who doesn't) http://www.suite101.com/content/digital-na-tives-and-digital-immigrants-a59935

➢ Read "aloud"; I'm not suggesting you recite your document to the entire office, just say the words quietly to yourself, this will slow you down and help you focus

➢ Short documents can be read backwards to check for spelling mistakes; I don't recommend this with the 300 page report though!

➢ And spellcheck – ah yes .....

83

CANDIDATE FOR A PULLET SURPRISE

I have a spelling checker,
It came with my PC.
It plane lee marks four my revue
Miss steaks aye can knot sea.

Eye ran this poem threw it,
Your sure reel glad two no.
Its vary polished in it's weigh.
My checker tolled me sew.

A checker is a bless sing,
It freeze yew lodes of thyme.
It helps me right awl stiles two reed,
And aides me when eye rime.

Each frays come posed up on my screen
Eye trussed too bee a joule.
The checker pours o'er every word
To cheque sum spelling rule.

Bee fore a veiling checker's
Hour spelling mite decline,
And if we're lacks oar have a laps,
We wood bee maid too wine.

Butt now bee cause my spelling
Is checked with such grate flare,
Their are know fault's with in my cite,
Of nun eye am a wear.

Now spelling does knot phase me,
It does knot bring a tier.
My pay purrs awl due glad den
With wrapped word's fare as hear.

To rite with care is quite a feet
Of witch won should bee proud,
And wee mussed dew the best wee can,
Sew flaw's are knot aloud.

Sow ewe can sea why aye dew prays
Such soft wear four pea seas,
And why eye brake in two averse
Buy righting want too pleas.

Written by Jerrold Zar and reprinted
with kind permission of
The Journal of Irreproducible Results,
The science humor magazine, www.jir.
com

Jarold Zar

Need I say more .....

What helps you check carefully?

Common mistakes

There can be so many opportunities for error in business documents, but I thought I'd go over some of the more common areas; it's not just about spelling mistakes.

Tautology

The first one I want to mention is tautology, which basically means saying the same thing twice, but usually with different words and, therefore, it is less noticeable. For example, I've often seen emails which say things like "I will revert back to you next week", "this is an essential prerequisite" or "the reason is because".

"Revert" means to go back to or return; therefore, "to revert back" is tautology, the back is superfluous. A "prerequisite" is something that is required and, therefore, essential is not needed.

A phrase such as "cheapest price" is tautology as the word "cheap" implies price. You should, therefore, write either "the cheapest" or "the lowest price". One of the most common is referring to a "PIN number"; PIN = personal identification number.

> Correct these examples of tautology:
>
> 1. In my opinion I believe that these are too expensive.
> 2. It is a necessary requirement that you complete this form.
> 3. I don't know the reason why he does that.
> 4. We walked into the room simultaneously at the same time.
> 5. If you are the first to apply you will receive a free gift.

You can find many more examples at http://www.buzzle.com/articles/tautology-examples.html .

Either/neither

The next common mistake is the incorrect use of either/or and neither/nor. Very simply, if you use either then use or; if you use neither then use nor.

Homophones

Our next area is homophones. These are words that sound the same, or similar, but are spelt differently. Here are some examples:

Sees, seize, seas (cease)

Cell, sell

Higher, hire

Discreet, discrete

And how about:

Right, write, rite, wright!

For lots more examples visit http://www.bifroest.demon.co.uk/misc/homophones-list.html .

You can also do a homophones quiz online at http://www.bbc.co.uk/skillswise/words/spelling/recognising/homophones/quiz.shtml

ise or ize

Watch also for lack of consistency with spelling – either use recognise and organise or recognize and organize – don't mix them (both are correct).

There is a misconception that using the z is American and the s English; that can be the case nowadays, but actually a z was originally used in Britain and this went with the first travellers to the US and was maintained there whereas it is used less in the UK.

And, obviously, check for spelling errors

Where to put the word both?

The cars were available both in red and black x

The cars were available in both red and black √

The cars were available both in red and in black √

Check for the following common punctuation errors:

Not closing brackets or quotation marks.

Wrongly placed punctuation – if a sentence starts outside a bracket, it should end outside; if it starts within the brackets, it should finish within. It is the same for quotation marks.

Commas never go between a subject and a verb (eg, "he said he, would do it" is wrong).

> Exercise: Insert commas where appropriate:
>
> 1. After a hard day at the office I like to relax with a cup of tea.
> 2. The recipe needed jam flour sugar fruit eggs and baking powder.
> 3. "There are exams in progress" he whispered.
> 4. Paulina a hard working student had decided to go and study in Greece.
> 5. As the snow continued to fall Karen thought she ought to leave work.
> 6. She was intelligent not especially practical.
> 7. Steven his head still spinning walked out of the office for the last time.

> Exercise: Are these commas correct? If not, where should they be? Should there be any more or fewer?
>
> 1. My favourite countries are, Spain, Greece, India, and Hungary.
>
> 2. Jill, a talented woman in the world of education decided to apply for the role of principal.
>
> 3. As you are, aware in the accommodation block kitchens may be shared.

Verbs and subjects

Another error that is easy to make is not putting the correct verb with a subject, for example:

✗ The group are working well.

✓ The group is working well.

A group is singular and therefore the second version is correct. You could, however, say "the members of the group are working well". If you are unsure replace "the group" with "it" and that will tell you whether it should be singular or plural. Similarly, replace "members" with "they" and that will help too.

✓ A basket of flowers is delivered.

✓ Flowers are delivered.

✓ The team is playing well.

However, it is correct to say:

The police are attending the event (you can't have the polices).

Similarly, despite what the word processing system tells you, "the staff are busy" is correct (we don't say "the staffs").

Also, if you use none, remember you should write "none is" not "none are" as none is short for not one.

Exercise: Have a go at inserting the correct verb in these sentences:

1. A box of files are/is on the shelf.

2. I think the team play/plays well.

3. The members of the committee vote/votes on the issue.

4. My friend and I like/likes ice skating.

5. The student group work/works hard.

Hyphens

Hyphens, in my opinion, should be avoided, unless their presence avoids ambiguity. They should also never be used with words ending in –ly (eg, environmentally friendly, newly arrived, etc).

You may need to differentiate between 20 odd MPs and 20-odd MPs! Equally, extra curricular activities are more activities within the curriculum, whereas extra-curricular activities are activities outside the curriculum. The same applies to extra marital sex ......

A word such as shell-like needs it to avoid the triple L. No-one really needs a hyphen as noone looks odd. I get round this by using nobody. If you do use hyphens, make sure you are consistent.

Apostrophes

Watch out for misplaced apostrophes. See the section on good English.

Comparatives and superlatives

Another common mistake is the misuse of comparatives and superlatives. For example, if you are comparing two things, one is the better, not the best; something can only be the best of three or more things.

This dress is the better of the two.

This suit is the best in the shop.

I have two daughters; one is the elder, the other is the younger.

Of the two mountains, Sca Fell is the higher.

Everest is the highest mountain in the world.

> Exercise: Insert the correct word.
> 1. Of the three suggestions, I think yours is the better/best.
> 2. I have a twin sister; she is the elder/eldest.
> 3. My friend and I bought identical bracelets but mine was the cheaper/cheapest.
> 4. Of all the many hotels in which I have stayed this has to be worse/the worst.

Less and fewer

How about less and fewer? How many people flinch as they read "5 items or less" at the supermarket checkout? Well you should! It's incorrect grammar ..... it should be "5 items or fewer".

It's all to do with countable and uncountable nouns and, before you doze off, this is very simple. A noun is countable if you can count it – for example, 1 bottle, 2 bottles, 3 bottles. Bottle is a countable noun. Milk, however, is not (1 milk, 2 milks, 3 milks – I don't think so).

If your noun is countable you should use fewer (items can be counted and, therefore, you should say "fewer items"), if it is uncountable you should use less (there is less milk in the jug than I thought).

Exercise: Have a go at this quiz:		
	Countable	Uncountable
Boy		
Girl		
Air		
Water		
Student		
Money		
Desk		
Milk		
Car		
Chair		
House		
Information		
Advice		
Heat		

Use "less" for uncountable nouns and "fewer" for countable nouns.

> ### Exercise: Insert "less" or "fewer" as appropriate:
>
> 1. There were .... students at the university last year.
> 2. I made .... mistakes this time.
> 3. Our department needs to spend .... money on stationery.
> 4. There were .... complications this time.
> 5. I've been there .... times than I should.
> 6. It was .... difficult than I thought it would be.
> 7. There are .... items on his list.

Me or I

Do some of you remember "The Two Ronnies" on TV a few years ago; the wonderful Ronnie Barker with Ronnie Corbett and their amazingly clever sketches and songs (what a wordsmith Ronnie Barker was!)? They used to end the show with "And it's goodnight from me.... and it's goodnight from him". How many of us think the Queen is correct always to say "my husband and I"? She is.....sometimes.

This is again a very simple rule: if you use me if you are on your own, you use me if you are with someone else; if you use I when you are on your own, you use I if you are with someone else too.

Would you like to come to the cinema with me?

Would you like to come to the cinema with my husband and me?

I would love you to come with us.

My husband and I would love you to come with us.

Word alternatives

(See the section on good English for more details.)

Watch out from words that can catch us out with their usage:

Different from, but dissimilar to

To compose of, but to comprise, eg, "our team is composed of experts in their field" or "our team comprises experts in their field"

Continual (happens repeatedly, but not constantly) and continuous (uninterrupted)

Practical (can be done and is worth doing) and practicable (can be done whether or not it is worth it)

And, of course, the verb/noun issue:

Practise/practice (always practice in US spelling)

Advise/advice

License/licence (always license in US spelling)

Affect/effect

Be careful of double letters sometimes, but not always, used in words:

Targeted, combating, skilful, fulfil (all correct)

Focussing and focusing are both correct, but always be consistent.

For further reading I suggest "Troublesome Words" by Bill Bryson

Repetition

Look out for too much repetition in your work; using the same words often and close together. Try and vary your vocabulary; use a Thesaurus to look for synonyms. Alternatively, you can simply use the word processing shortcut (select a word by double clicking on it, right click in the highlighted area and select "synonyms" from the shortcut menu). The book is usually better though.

Ambiguity

A final common mistake is ambiguity in texts. We often type things and presume they're OK because we know what we want to say. However, it may not be clear to the reader:

The chair was by the table when I fixed it (fixed what, the table or the chair?).

Exercise: Have a go at correcting this paragraph:

When you are checking your work it, is important to ensure the punctuation is in the correct place. Me and my colleague always make an attempt to try and get it right. In fact, I do this both at at work and home. It has a good affect on the way I present my work. Last week my boss said, "I am really pleased with the standard of your work." (This made me very happy). I hope this will improve my future prospects.

Word order

The word order in your sentences can be vital; it is easy to change the meaning of a phrase just by putting a word in the wrong place.

> Exercise: See how many different meanings you can give this sentence by adding the word "only" in as many places as possible. (Written by John Humphrys)
>
> The Prime Minister listens to the Chancellor's advice.

Foreign phrases

Only use foreign phrases where there is no English equivalent available.

We've spoken about checking for good English but don't forget we use at lot of foreign phrases in our business writing (ad hoc, pro forma, etc).

I have no problem with these being used, where appropriate, but overuse can look ridiculous and pompous. If a phrase is not yet considered part of the English language it should be written in italics.

Here are some more examples:

➤ *Ad nauseam* - to the point of disgust
➤ *Bona fide* - in good faith, authentic
➤ *Carte blanche* - a free hand
➤ *Curriculum vitae* - course of one's life; a resume
➤ *Fait accompli* - something already done [usually used with the hidden meaning that opposition is useless]
➤ *Laissez faire* - a policy of non-interference
➤ *Pro rata* - in proportion
➤ *Vice versa* - the other way around; conversely

You can find many more examples at http://www.infoplease.com/ipa/A0001619.html .

To finish, here are some examples of what can happen when people don't check carefully:

➢ Toilet out of order ... please use floor below

➢ Automatic washing machine: please remove all your clothes when the light goes out

➢ Bargain basement upstairs

➢ After tea break staff should empty the teapot and stand upside down on the draining board

➢ For anyone who has children and doesn't know it, there is a day care centre on the 1st floor

Chapter 9:
Persuasive communication

"Before you try to convince anyone else,
be sure you are convinced, and
if you cannot convince yourself, drop the subject."
John Henry Patterson

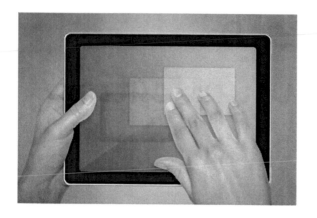

Chapter 9:
Persuasive communication

In this chapter you will learn:

- ✓ How to ask for something
- ✓ What business clichés to avoid
- ✓ How to offer solutions and incentives
- ✓ Turning bad news into good news
- ✓ Use of appropriate and positive language

I wrote earlier about how important preparation is to producing successful and effective correspondence. Not just preparing your text and content, but also thinking about your reader. The next step is when you want to write persuasively.

If you want to persuade someone then ask them in the way they'd like to be asked not how you'd like to be asked.

So many of our communications are to ask for information, to get things done, to arrange events, to obtain payment, etc. We are attempting to persuade people to do something for us – basically we need to market our idea.

Here are 6 ways you can do this:

1. High standards

As soon as a person opens a letter or email which is badly written they will not be favourable to helping the writer.

Always ensure your correspondence is of the highest standard – this will impress.

2. Avoiding clichés

It is lazy, unimaginative and boring to rely on hackneyed business phrases which go back to the 1950s. We are in the 21st century now and should write as such. I do not mean use text-speak or ignoring apostrophes, all these standards continue to be vital. However, we do express ourselves differently, people are more natural nowadays and the formality of bygone times is no longer relevant ..... you wouldn't think so from some of the correspondence I see!

This is my all time "favourite" cliché: "if you have any queries, please do not hesitate to contact me". You see it everywhere, everyone uses it and it has therefore lost its impact. It doesn't sound as though you care at all, it sounds as though you have no ideas of your own.

The definition of a cliché is an expression or idea that has become trite (with trite meaning worn out by constant use; no longer having freshness, originality, or novelty; stale). You know how it ends when it starts.

There are so many different ways we could write this and still sound polite:

➢ Do give me a call if you have any questions
➢ Let me know if you need any more information
➢ Feel free to send me any queries you may have

Exercise: Business cliché hunt, keep your ears and eyes open for clichés over the next week.

The more you vary your phrases, the more impact your correspondence will have.

Make every effort to avoid phrases such as "I am writing" – talk about stating the obvious!

"It was nice to meet you" – my goodness, I'm overwhelmed by your excitement. Why not sometimes be delighted to have met someone. We are not delighted enough nowadays ....

Basically, the more you can vary the way you write, the more you will be able to persuade your reader.

Watch out for your own clichés!

Exercise: Here are some other examples of clichéd business phrases; suggest some alternatives:

Above mentioned	
and as requested write to advise you that	
We enclose herewith	
Your account in our books	
Our above named customer	
Perhaps you would be kind enough to	
Prior to	
Subsequent to	
At this moment in time	
We wonder whether you will be so kind as to	
We write with reference to	

3. WIIFM - What's In It For Me?

Do you remember when word processing was first being used? We started to receive letters (obviously circulars) addressed to us personally – mail merge had arrived. The catalogue companies told us we were their favourite customer and they had special offers just for us. It was quite exciting at first, until we realised everyone got these letters; but, for a while, we thought there was something for us....

So, can we use this today to try and persuade people to give us information, provide us with help, etc? We can try.

A few years ago I worked with a double glazing company who were disappointed with the results they were getting from their mailings. I had a look at the letter they were circulating, which was well written. However, the letter first of all introduced the company and the directors and told the reader how high standards were important to them and that they were a family business, etc, etc. By this time the reader may well have thrown the letter in the waste bin. At the end, in the last paragraph, almost an afterthought, they had written "... and if you install our windows in your factory, it can save you £30,000 a year on heating bills."

Now that's what we want to know. That statement should have opened the letter: "Dear Sir/Madam, We can save you £30,000 a year on your heating bills." That will get your reader's attention. You can then continue to outline your standards and write about your history, which will serve to reinforce the interest you have immediately raised.

When a Sales Manager wanted his reps to give him their monthly figures so he could write a report for his Director, they were all too busy. When he reframed the question and asked for the figures so he could calculate their bonuses, you can imagine the very different response!

It's not always possible to find something, but always try.

4. Offering solutions

If you send emails to people with lots of questions and problems they will feel overwhelmed and stressed and not necessarily open to helping you.

Try instead to send emails giving your reader(s) viable solutions – particularly if you are writing to management.

5. Turning bad news into good news

It is very easy, when we anticipate our reader's reaction, to actually cause that reaction.

If we expect the recipient to be unhappy about something we are writing, we use negative and apologetic language and can, therefore, actually exacerbate the situation.

Using phrases like "unfortunately", "We are sorry to report", etc immediately make the reader on edge.

Incidentally, only apologise if you are at fault; otherwise there are risks of accepting liability. You can always say "I am sorry to read of your problem" or "I am sorry you are unhappy with the service".

Look at this example:

Unfortunately, we are sorry to tell you that the information you need will not be available for at least 2 hours. We apologise for the inconvenience this may cause you (cliché alert!!).

Perhaps you could have written:

We are pleased to confirm that the information you need will be available within 3 hours and if we can get it to you sooner we will do.

This is called "reframing" and is generally a good principle; it's seeing the glass half full rather than half empty. It does ensure a better reaction from your reader.

Exercise: Have a go at re-writing these examples:	
I regret to inform you that your admission to candidate status has been delayed until you complete the following requirements:	
On 3 March, we sent you the claim forms and requested that you return them to us. It is now 27 March and we have not yet received your reply.	
Due to the work involved in building the new canteen, I'm afraid there will be no restaurant facilities available this week.	
Unfortunately, you have failed your examination and you won't be able to resit this for at least a month.	

6. Use of appropriate vocabulary

An important part of your planning should also be thinking about the words that you use. As an NLP (neuro-linguistic programming) practitioner, I have the pleasure of helping PAs and administrators to find ways to improve their relationships with colleagues and build rapport with others. These techniques can transfer to written communication too.

For written communication the language level is vital. Very simply, speaking the same language as another person brings you closer, but there is more to it than that, even when we speak the same language as the other person.

Do you have dinner, supper or tea? Do you have a lounge, living room, sitting room, front room, parlour or drawing room? Do you have a sofa, a couch, a settee or a chaise-longue? All these words give away a great deal about our background and we automatically "warm" to people who use the same words as we do.

How much more effective then would it be to use the same words as your reader?
How much more persuasive could you be?

We can take this a step further; it is possible to build rapport with different types of people. This is done at 4 levels:

➤ non-verbal – body language and eye contact

➤ tone of voice

➤ language – not just speaking the same language, but also using the same types of words (more shortly)

➤ beliefs – not just religion, but also ethics, standards, interests, etc

We start building rapport with a person the second we meet them; we "connect" with people who walk and stand as we do, who make eye contact as we do. This then moves on to the level of tone of voice – quiet people aren't happy with loud people, for example; rapport would be difficult. We then move to the levels of language and beliefs.

I mentioned earlier, if you use similar words to a person, you will build rapport with that person. You can also develop this by being aware of representational systems. We gather information through our senses (sight, hearing, feeling, taste and smell) and we all have preferences in the way we use these – the first three being the main ones.

Our preferences can be reflected in the vocabulary we use so, for example, a visual person may say "I see what you mean", whereas an auditory person could say "that sounds interesting". Someone whose preferred system is with feelings (kinaesthetic) may say "How do you feel about that?"

A means to build rapport with somebody is by using the same types of words they use. If you can pick out their preference from their vocabulary you can start to use similar phrases. Of course, this can extend to writing. Listen to people and use their words in communications with them. If you haven't met them, read their correspondence carefully and see if you can pick up their preferences and mirror them in your replies.

It has been suggested that this technique is manipulation; I would say that it is only manipulation if you are persuading somebody to do something wrong or hurtful. If, in the long run, everyone benefits, then it can only be for the best.

Going back to turning bad news into good, always try and use positive words and, wherever possible, use "and" instead of "but". This is particularly important if you are writing to someone with feedback on their performance ...

"You've done a really good job, BUT ....." Oh dear, that deflates our reader completely. How much better to write "You've done a really good job and, once the parking problems are sorted, everything will be excellent."

Finally, watch out for that little word "just" that slips in so easily. "I just do the filing," "I just work for the MD," and my favourite, "I'm just a secretary!"

Chapter 10:
Action plan and check list

"Success will never be a big step in the future, success is a small step taken just now." Jonatan Mårtensson

Chapter 10:
Action plan and checklist

In this chapter you will:

✓ Get a check list for your written communication

✓ Create an action plan for your continuing development

Now you have so many tools to enable you to write excellent and effective correspondence and reports, you need to write up an action plan with specific goals; in this way changes will happen.

You must ensure that your actions are specific – so, for example, saying "I will improve my business writing" is not good enough; you have to decide what specifically you are going to do. For example, "I will visit grammar websites to improve my use of apostrophes" or "I will check all emails to ensure I have not used negative words where they are not needed".

You can also give yourself deadlines to achieve these improvements.

Action plan

Having worked through the book, have a think about either actions to do with writing or for further training. Be very specific about each one and give them a date so that you can tick them off as you achieve them.

Action	Date to be achieved

ACTION PLAN

Action	Date to be achieved

Final checklist for any writing you do:

- ❑ Clarity, accuracy, consistency
- ❑ Proofreading
- ❑ Convey a good image
- ❑ Consider the recipient – background, knowledge, culture
- ❑ No superfluous information
- ❑ Loyalty to your organisation and colleagues
- ❑ Good spelling, punctuation and grammar
- ❑ Tone and style
- ❑ W.I.I.F.M. and persuasion
- ❑ 4 point plan; open, detail, what happens next, close
- ❑ Economy of words
- ❑ Short sentences, but not too abrupt
- ❑ Stick to the facts
- ❑ Are all facts accurate?
- ❑ Have all typing errors been corrected?
- ❑ Have you included all information?
- ❑ Is the information up to date?
- ❑ Is there enough information?
- ❑ Does the reader know what he/she needs to do?
- ❑ Are all contact details included?
- ❑ Would you be proud to sign your name on this document?
- ❑ And, of course, NEVER send anything if you are angry or inebriated!

And finally....

In the introduction I outlined why I think excellence in business writing is so vital; I also said that language should be allowed to evolve. Part of that evolution is making the choice to go back to plain English, to making life easier for your reader and to getting the best results for everyone concerned.

It is said "if what you're doing isn't working – do something else"; I cannot agree more. I hope that now you've read this book you will choose to excel.

If you want to contact me please either email Heather@uolearn.com or visit my website www.bakerthompsonassoc.co.uk.

Best of luck with your writing,

Heather

Answers

Page 34

1. I hope to hear from you soon.	What happens next?
2. We are pleased to inform you that our Banquet Suite is available on the dates you require.	Detail
3. Thank you for your letter of	Opening
4. I am pleased to enclose our latest catalogue.	Detail
5. Do let me know if you have any questions.	What happens next?

Page 59

<u>Verbs</u>, underlined, **nouns** bold and adjectives grey.

1. The usual **chairperson** <u>read</u> the **minutes**.

2. It <u>was agreed</u> to <u>increase</u> the annual **salaries**.

3. **Mr Smith** <u>volunteered</u> to <u>send</u> an explanatory **email**.

4. **KL** <u>said</u> that **he** <u>would try out</u> the new **system**.

Page 61

1. He had been **practicing(US) practising(UK)** medicine for years.
2. It was a nice **compliment** about my work.
3. The **principal** reason why the project succeeded was the team management.
4. The chairperson was concerned about the **effect** this would have on the **practice** time.

Page 66

1. The clients' rooms are nearby.
2. The manager's response was "no".
3. The secretaries' attitude must improve.
4. The men's preference was to sit down.
5. The caretaker says that he's happy with this plan.
6. You're not sure what your choice will be.
7. It's difficult to know if the company and its representatives are included.
8. The SATs were very difficult.

Page 67

It was agreed that the manager would probably outline her plans to the department. The chairperson reported the CEO's comment that everyone should be told of the likelihood of redundancies. She added that she concurred with this.

Page 71

At the meeting today the Chief Executive, Mr John Smith, suggested that a training course should be held for all sales staff. Members agreed that a two day seminar would be most appropriate; it will be held in October. It is, therefore, important that you and I should meet to decide on topics. Suggestions for speakers will also be needed. Of course, your expertise and help in making the arrangements will be very valuable. Please let me know when it will be convenient for us to meet; any afternoon next week would be suitable for me.
OR

At the meeting today the Chief Executive, Mr John Smith, suggested that a training course should be held for all sales staff. Members agreed that a two day seminar would be most appropriate. It will be held in October, it is, therefore, important that you and I should meet to decide on topics. Suggestions for speakers will also be needed, of course. Your expertise and help in making the arrangements will be very valuable. Please let me know when it will be convenient for us to meet. Any afternoon next week would be suitable for me.

Page 72

1. The statements will be sent to you on 12 July.

2. Unfortunately I am unable to accept your kind invitation.

3. Please find enclosed a copy of our latest terms and conditions.

4. Thank you for your letter of 8 January.

ANSWERS

Page 73

Come to a decision	Decide
In the event that	If
Commence	Start/begin
Terminate	End/finish
At the present moment in time	Now/currently
Due to the fact that	Because
It is possible that	Possibly
It is probable that	Probably
For the purpose of	For

Page 74

1. Although it was circling over the bathers, the shark-spotting helicopter apparently failed to see shark.

2. As the guard went about his duties the older prisoner watched him closely, noting the time he came to feed the new arrival.

3. I told my manager that Mrs Jones should help her colleague.

4. Boil the milk if the baby doesn't like it cold.

5. There are some sticking plasters, which I keep for emergencies, in my desk.

6. When I painted the car it was in the garage.

Page 76

1. This is rude and makes, possibly incorrect, assumptions. The letter may have just gone missing in the system.
I have not yet received a reply to my letter.

2. It may not be your problem, but it is totally inappropriate to say that to a client. A helpful attitude will enhance the image of you and your organisation.
Unfortunately we are unable to help with your problem. We suggest you call a solicitor and can recommend ......

3. This really does sound like "be there or die"! People should be invited to interviews; you want the prospective employees to really want to work with you.
We would like to invite you to an interview on Tuesday 20 May at 2pm.

4. Again, a totally inappropriate tone to use to anyone. Unfortunately, though, sometimes it is clearly the person's fault. A good way to get around this is to use phrases that, what I call, "float in the air".
This problem can arise if the funds are not transferred correctly.

We're not implying it's their fault, but telling them what may cause the problem. A more subtle way of telling them it's their fault!

5. This may be true but, phrased in this way, it comes across as rather aggressive.
As your policy has expired, there will be a charge for the repairs.

Remember, no apologies are needed if it's not your fault or just a fact. Don't apologise too much. You have to be careful, too, of admitting liability.

6. Similar to number 4, this is very accusing. Try the "float in the air" style here.
We're sorry to hear that your DVD player doesn't work. This can happen if it hasn't been wired correctly.

You're not apologising for the fact it doesn't work, but you're sorry to hear they have a problem.

ANSWERS

Page 85

1. I believe that these are too expensive. or
   In my opinion, these are too expensive.

2. It is a requirement that you complete this form. or
   It is necessary that you complete this form

3. I don't know why he does that. or
   I don't know the reason he does that

4. We walked into the room simultaneously. or
   We walked into the room at the same time

5. If you are the first to apply you will receive a gift

Page 87

1. After a hard day at the office, I like to relax with a cup of tea.

2. The recipe needed jam, flour, sugar, fruit, eggs and baking powder.

3. "There are exams in progress," he whispered.

4. Paulina, a hard working student, had decided to go and study in Greece.

5. As the snow continued to fall, Karen thought she ought to leave work.

6. She was intelligent, not especially practical.

7. Steven, his head still spinning, walked out of the office for the last time.

Page 88

1. My favourite countries are Spain, Greece, India and Hungary.

2. Jill, a talented woman in the world of education, decided to apply for the role of principal.

3. As you are aware, in the accommodation block, kitchens may be shared.

Page 89

1. A box of files **is** on the shelf.
2. I think the team **plays** well.
3. The members of the committee **vote** on the issue.
4. My friend and I **like** ice skating.
5. The student group **works** hard.

Page 90

Of the three suggestions, I think yours is the **best**.

I have a twin sister; she is the **elder.**

My friend and I bought identical bracelets but mine was the **cheaper**.

Of all the many hotels in which I have stayed this has to be **the worst.**

Page 91

	Countable	Uncountable
Boy	Yes	
Girl	Yes	
Air		Yes
Water		Yes
Student	Yes	
Money		Yes
Desk	Yes	
Car	Yes	
Chair	Yes	
House	Yes	
Information		Yes
Advice		Yes
Heat		Yes

Page 92

1. There were **fewer** students at the university last year.

2. I made **fewer** mistakes this time.

3. Our department needs to spend **less** money on stationery.

4. There were **fewer** complications this time.

5. I've been there **fewer** times than I should.

6. It was **less** difficult than I thought it would be.

7. There are **fewer** items on his list.

Page 94

When you are checking your work, it is important to ensure the punctuation is in the correct place. My colleague and I always try and get it right. In fact, I do this both at work and at home. It has a good effect on the way I present my work. Last week my boss said, "I am really pleased with the standard of your work". (This made me very happy.) I hope this will improve my prospects.

Did you spot the two examples of tautology?

Page 95

Only the Prime Minister listens to the Chancellor's advice.

The **only** Prime Minister listens to the Chancellor's advice.

The Prime Minister **only** listens to the Chancellor's advice.

The Prime Minister listens **only** to the Chancellor's advice.

The Prime Minister listens to **only** the Chancellor's advice.

The Prime Minister listens to the **only** Chancellor's advice.

The Prime Minister listens to the Chancellor's **only** advice.

The Prime Minister listens to the Chancellor's advice **only**.

8 versions with at least 5 different meanings.

(with thanks to John Humphrys' "Lost for Words")

Page 101

Abovementioned	above
and as requested write to advise you that	and are pleased to inform you
We enclose herewith	We enclose
Your account in our books	Your account
Our above named customer	Our customer (or the customer's name)
Perhaps you would be kind enough to	Would you please We would appreciate
Prior to	Before
Subsequent to	After
At this moment in time	Currently Now
We wonder whether you will be so kind as to	Could you possibly
We write with reference to	With reference to Further to

Page 104

I regret to inform you that your admission to candidate status has been delayed until you complete the following requirements:	I am pleased to tell you that, as soon as you have completed the following requirements, you will be admitted to candidate status.
On 3 March, we sent you the claim forms and requested that you return them to us. It is now 27 March and we have not yet received your reply.	To enable us to settle your claim and arrange payment, please could you return the completed forms by return.
Due to the work involved in building the new canteen, I'm afraid there will be no restaurant facilities available this week.	We are delighted to announce that your newly refurbished canteen will be open next week and, in the meantime, we have arranged for sandwiches to be delivered.
Unfortunately, you have failed your examination and you won't be able to resit this for at least a month.	Although you have not passed your examination, we are pleased to confirm that you will be able to resit this within the next 6 weeks.

Universe of
Learning Books

"The purpose of learning is growth, and our
minds, unlike our bodies, can continue growing
as we continue to live." Mortimer Adler

About the publishers

Universe of Learning Limited is a small publisher based in the UK with production in England, Australia and America. Our authors are all experienced trainers or teachers who have taught their skills for many years. We are actively seeking qualified authors and if you visit the authors section on www.uolearn.com you can find out how to apply.

If you are interested in any of our current authors (including Heather Baker) coming to speak at your event please do visit their own websites (to contact Heather please email heather@ uolearn.com, website www.bakerthompsonassoc.co.uk) or email them through the author section of the uolearn site.

If you would like to purchase larger numbers of books then please do contact us (sales@uolearn.com). We give discounts from 5 books upwards. For larger volumes we can also quote for changes to the cover to accommodate your company logo and to the interior to brand it for your company.

All our books are written by teachers, trainers or people well experienced in their roles and our goal is to help people develop their skills with a well structured range of exercises.

If you have any feedback about this book or other topics that you'd like to see us cover please do contact us at support@uolearn.com.

To buy the printed books please order from your favourite bookshop, including Amazon, Waterstones, Blackwells and Barnes and Noble. For ebooks please visit www.uolearn.com.

Keep Learning!

Speed Writing

Speedwriting for faster
note taking and dictation

ISBN 978-1-84937-011-0, from www.uolearn.com

Easy exercises to learn faster writing in just 6 hours.

✓ "The principles are very easy to follow, and I am already using it to take notes."
✓ "I will use this system all the time."
✓ "Your system is so easy to learn and use."

Report Writing

An easy to follow format
for writing reports

ISBN 978-1-84937-036-3, from www.uolearn.com

This book makes report writing a step by step process for you to follow every time you have a report to write.

✓ How to set objectives using 8 simple questions
✓ Easy to follow flow chart
✓ How to write an executive summary
✓ How to layout and structure the report
✓ Help people remember what they read

Successful Minute Taking
Meeting the Challenge

How to prepare, write and organise
agendas and minutes of meetings

ISBN 978-1-84937-040-0, from www.uolearn.com

✓ Becoming more confident in your role
✓ A checklist of what to do
✓ Help with layout and writing skills
✓ Learn what to include in minutes
✓ How to work well with your chairperson

Learn to be an excellent meeting secretary.

STUDY SKILLS, BECOMING A TUTOR, DREAM INTERPRETATION

Studying for your Future

Skills for life, whilst you study

ISBN: 978-1-84937-047-9, Order at www.uolearn.com

- ✓ A checklist to put together a portfolio to show a prospective employer
- ✓ Learn the skills to prepare you for your degree
- ✓ Help you with literature reviews and writing skills
- ✓ Goal setting to help you focus on your future
- ✓ Sort out your time planning
- ✓ Improve your study skills and exam preparation
- ✓ Prepare for employment

How to Start a Business as a Private Tutor

ISBN 978-1-84937-029-5, from www.uolearn.com

This book, by a Lancashire based author, shows you how to set up your own business as a tutor.

- ✓ Packed with tips and stories
- ✓ How to get started - what to do and buy
- ✓ How to attract clients and advertise
- ✓ Free printable forms, ready to use
- ✓ Advice on preparing students for exams

Dreaming Yourself Aware

Exercises to interpret your dreams

ISBN: 978-1-84937-055-4, Order at www.uolearn.com

- ✓ Learn how to remember and record your dreams
- ✓ Structured approach to understand your dreams
- ✓ A large variety of techniques for dream interpretation
- ✓ Step by step instructions and worked examples
- ✓ Exercises to help you to find answers to problems
- ✓ Understand your motivation and reveal your goals
- ✓ Make positive changes to your life

Dreaming yourself aware gives a step by step guide to interpreting your dreams.

126

Coaching Skills Training Course

Business and life coaching techniques for

ISBN: 978-1-84937-019-6, from www.uolearn.com
- ✓ An easy to follow 5 step model
- ✓ Learn to both self-coach and coach others
- ✓ Over 25 ready to use ideas
- ✓ Goal setting tools to help achieve ambitions

A toolbox of ideas to help you become a great coach.

Stress Management

Exercises and techniques to manage stress and anxiety

ISBN: 978-1-84937-002-8, from www.uolearn.com
- ✓ Understand what stress is
- ✓ Become proactive in managing your stress
- ✓ How to become more positive about your life
- ✓ An easy 4 step model to lasting change

Practical and Effective Performance Management

ISBN: 978-1-84937-037-0, from www.uolearn.com
- ✓ Five key ideas to understanding performance
- ✓ A clear four step model
- ✓ Key what works research that is practical
- ✓ A large, wide ranging choice of tools
- ✓ Practical exercises and action planning for managers

A toolbox of ideas to help you become a better leader.

Developing Your Influencing Skills

ISBN: 978-1-84937-004-2, from www.uolearn.com
- ✓ Decide what your influencing goals are
- ✓ Find ways to increase your credibility rating
- ✓ Develop stronger and more trusting relationships
- ✓ Inspire others to follow your lead
- ✓ Become a more influential communicator

Packed with case studies, exercises and practical tips to become more influential.

"Then there's the joy of getting your desk clean,
and knowing that all your letters are answered,
and you can see the wood on it again."
Lady Bird Johnson

Lightning Source UK Ltd.
Milton Keynes UK
UKOW021401231012

201044UK00003B/36/P